THE
BOOK
OF
DANIEL

THE
BOOK
OF
DANIEL

ILLUMINATED
BY
MARY BREEDEN

ELDERBERRY PRESS, INC.
1393 Old Homestead Drive, Second Floor
Oakland, Oregon 97462-9506.
E-MAIL: editor@elderberrypress. com
TEL/FAX: 541. 459. 6043
www. elderberrypress. com

Red Anvil books are available from your favorite bookstore, amazon. com, or from our 24 hour order line: 1. 800. 431. 1579

Publisher's Catalog-in-Publication Data
The Book of Daniel/Mary Breeden
ISBN 1932762264
1. Bible.
2. Book of Daniel.
3. Daniel.
4. Illuminated Manuscripts.
5. Illuminated Text.
I. Title
This book was written, printed and bound in the United States of America.

FOR MY GRANDCHILDREN
ANN, KATHLEEN, ELAINE,
CAROLINE, MARY CLAIRE
AND MY HONORARY GRANDCHILD
ALICE

Chapter 1

In the third year of the reign of Jehoiakim King of Judah, Nebuchadnezzar King of Babylon marched on Jerusalem and beseiged it. The Lord delivered Jehoiakim King of Judah into his hands, along with some of the sacred vessels of the Temple of God. Nebuchadnezzar carried these

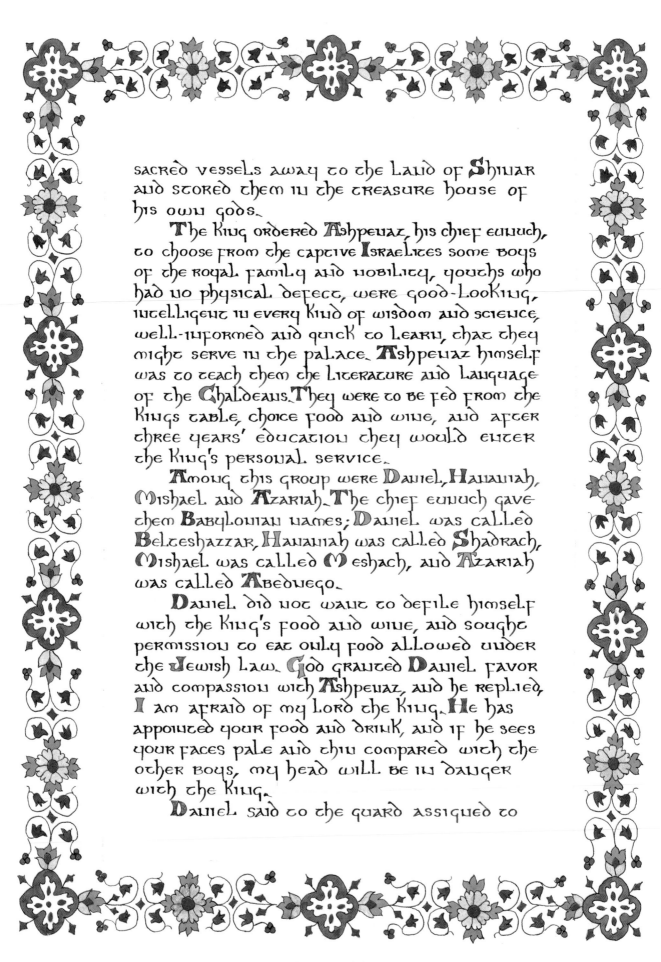

sacred vessels away to the land of Shinar and stored them in the treasure house of his own gods.

The King ordered Ashpenaz, his chief eunuch, to choose from the captive Israelites some boys of the royal family and nobility, youths who had no physical defect, were good-looking, intelligent in every kind of wisdom and science, well-informed and quick to learn, that they might serve in the palace. Ashpenaz himself was to teach them the literature and language of the Chaldeans. They were to be fed from the King's table, choice food and wine, and after three years' education they would enter the King's personal service.

Among this group were Daniel, Hananiah, Mishael and Azariah. The chief eunuch gave them Babylonian names; Daniel was called Belteshazzar, Hananiah was called Shadrach, Mishael was called Meshach, and Azariah was called Abednego.

Daniel did not want to defile himself with the King's food and wine, and sought permission to eat only food allowed under the Jewish law. God granted Daniel favor and compassion with Ashpenaz, and he replied, I am afraid of my lord the King. He has appointed your food and drink, and if he sees your faces pale and thin compared with the other boys, my head will be in danger with the King.

Daniel said to the guard assigned to

them, Please permit us to have a ten-day trial, during which we will eat only vegetables and water. You can then compare our faces with the faces of the boys who eat the king's food, and deal with us according to what you see. The man agreed to do what they asked, and tested them for ten days. At the end of the ten days, they looked better and healthier than any of the boys who had eaten at the royal table, so they were allowed to continue with their chosen diet.

God gave these four youths knowledge and skill in all learning and wisdom, and Daniel was given the gift of understanding and interpreting every kind of vision and dream.

When the training period of three years came to an end, Nebuchadnezzar ordered all the young men to be brought before him, and none could compare with Daniel, Hananiah, Mishael and Azariah. In every matter of wisdom and understanding they were ten times better than all the magicians and astrologers in his entire kingdom. So Daniel remained at the court until the first year of King Cyrus.

Chapter 2

In the second year of his reign, King Nebuchadnezzar dreamed dreams that troubled him, and he could not sleep. However, he could not remember his dreams. He called for his magicians and astrologers and sorcerers and Chaldeans to tell him what his dreams meant. They came and stood before him.

The King said, I have dreamed a dream and am troubled by a desire to understand it.

They answered the King, O King, live for ever. Tell your servants the dream, and we will give you the interpretation.

The King answered, The dream is gone from me. If you cannot tell me the dream and its interpretation, you will be cut in pieces and your houses destroyed. But if you reveal the dream and its meaning, I will give you gifts and rewards and great honor. So tell me what I dreamt and what it means.

They spoke the second time, Tell us the

dream, and we will give the interpretation.

The King said, It is clear to me that you are trying to gain time because you see that my orders are firm. You do not intend to interpret my dream, but to speak lies and delaying speeches until it is too late for me. Tell me the dream, and I will know that you have the correct interpretation.

The Chaldeans answered the King, There is not a man upon earth who could tell others what they  have dreamed. And there is no King or ruler who would ask such a thing of any magician, astrologer or Chaldean. What the King demands is difficult, and only the gods can reveal it, whose dwelling is not with mortal men.

At this the King flew into a rage, and gave orders that all the wise men of Babylon should be killed. The decree went forth, and they also sought to kill Daniel and his companions.

Daniel approached Arioch, the captain of the King's guard, and executioner, and spoke with great wisdom, saying, Why is this decree from the King so urgent?

Arioch informed Daniel about the matter, and Daniel went before the King and requested time to reveal his interpretation to the King. Then Daniel went home and told Hananiah, Meshach and Azariah what had happened. They asked the God of heaven to be merciful, and spare them the fate of the wise men of Babylon.

Then the mystery was revealed to Daniel in a night vision, and he praised the God of heaven, saying,

Blessed is the name of God for ever and ever, for wisdom and power are his;

He controls times and seasons;

He removes Kings and establishes Kings;

He gives wisdom to the wise and knowledge—

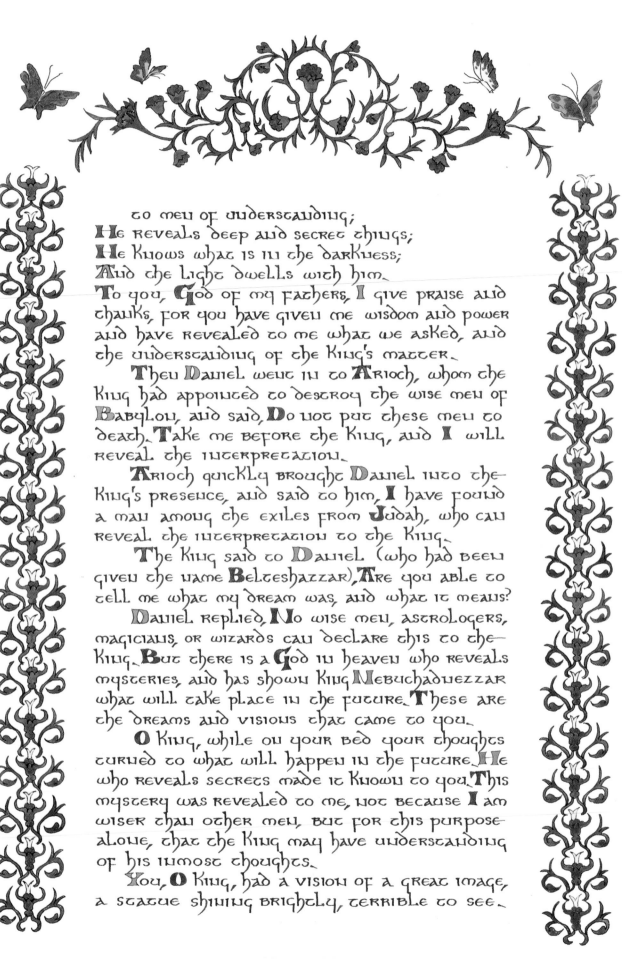

to men of understanding;
He reveals deep and secret things;
He knows what is in the darkness;
And the light dwells with him.
To you, God of my fathers, I give praise and thanks, for you have given me wisdom and power and have revealed to me what we asked, and the understanding of the king's matter.

Then Daniel went in to Arioch, whom the king had appointed to destroy the wise men of Babylon, and said, Do not put these men to death. Take me before the king, and I will reveal the interpretation.

Arioch quickly brought Daniel into the king's presence, and said to him, I have found a man among the exiles from Judah, who can reveal the interpretation to the king.

The king said to Daniel (who had been given the name Belteshazzar), Are you able to tell me what my dream was, and what it means?

Daniel replied, No wise men, astrologers, magicians, or wizards can declare this to the king. But there is a God in heaven who reveals mysteries, and has shown King Nebuchadnezzar what will take place in the future. These are the dreams and visions that came to you.

O king, while on your bed your thoughts turned to what will happen in the future. He who reveals secrets made it known to you. This mystery was revealed to me, not because I am wiser than other men, but for this purpose alone, that the king may have understanding of his inmost thoughts.

You, O king, had a vision of a great image, a statue shining brightly, terrible to see.

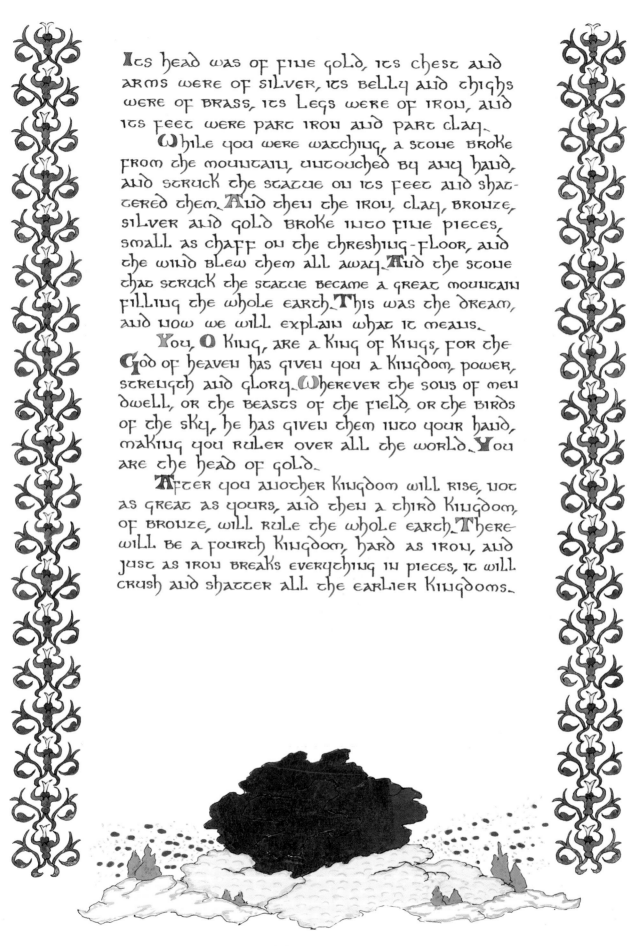

Its head was of fine gold, its chest and arms were of silver, its belly and thighs were of brass, its legs were of iron, and its feet were part iron and part clay.

While you were watching, a stone broke from the mountain, untouched by any hand, and struck the statue on its feet and shattered them. And then the iron, clay, bronze, silver and gold broke into fine pieces, small as chaff on the threshing-floor, and the wind blew them all away. And the stone that struck the statue became a great mountain filling the whole earth. This was the dream, and now we will explain what it means.

You, O King, are a King of Kings, for the God of heaven has given you a kingdom, power, strength and glory. Wherever the sons of men dwell, or the beasts of the field, or the birds of the sky, he has given them into your hand, making you ruler over all the world. You are the head of gold.

After you another kingdom will rise, not as great as yours, and then a third kingdom, of bronze, will rule the whole earth. There will be a fourth kingdom, hard as iron, and just as iron breaks everything in pieces, it will crush and shatter all the earlier kingdoms.

The feet that you saw, part iron and part clay, are a kingdom divided which retains part of its strength. They will try to strengthen themselves by joining together, but this will not succeed any better than iron will mix with clay.

In the time of these kings the God of heaven will set up a kingdom which will never be destroyed; no one will ever conquer it. It will shatter and consume all the previous kingdoms and it shall stand for ever. This is the meaning of the stone untouched by hand which broke from the mountain, and scattered the iron, clay, bronze, silver and gold. The great God has shown the king what will take place. The dream is true, and the interpretation trustworthy.

At this, King Nebuchadnezzar fell on his face before Daniel and worshiped him. He ordered sacrifices and sweet incense to be offered to Daniel. And the king said to Daniel, Truly your God is the God of gods, Ruler of kings, Revealer of mysteries, since you have revealed this secret.

The king gave Daniel a high position, and presented him with many costly gifts, and made him governor of the whole province of Babylon. At Daniel's request the king appointed Shadrach, Meshach and Abednego as his assistants in the affairs of the province of Babylon, and Daniel remained at the court of the king.

Chapter 3

King Nebuchadnezzar had a golden statue made, ninety feet high and nine feet wide, which he erected on the plain of Dura in the province of Babylon. Then he summoned the princes, governors, captains, judges, treasurers, counsellors and all the provincial rulers to the dedication of his statue. When they were assembled before the statue, a herald shouted this proclamation, O people of all nations and languages! This is the King's command! At the moment that you hear the sound of the horn, flute, harp, lyre, dulcimer, or any other musical instrument, you are to fall to the ground and worship the golden image that King Nebuchadnezzar has set up.

Anyone who does not prostrate himself and worship shall immediately be thrown into the burning fiery furnace. So when the music began, all of the people fell down and worshiped the golden statue.

At this time certain Chaldeans came forward and accused the Jews. They said to the King, O King, Live for ever. You have made a decree that every man who hears the sound of the music must fall on his face and worship the golden image that you have erected, and that anyone who does not do so will be thrown into the burning fiery furnace. However, there are certain Jews whom you have appointed as administrators in the affairs

of the province of Babylon, Shadrach, Meshach and Abednego. These men, O King, have ignored your command and have refused to worship the golden statue.

Nebuchadnezzar was very angry to hear this and sent for Shadrach, Meshach and Abednego. They were brought before the King.

He asked, Is it true that you do not serve my gods and refuse to worship the golden statue I set up? I will give you another chance. When you hear the sound of the musical instruments, you must fall to the ground and worship. If you do, all will be well. If you do not, you will immediately be thrown into the burning fiery furnace, and where is the god who can deliver you out of my hands?

Shadrach, Meshach and Abednego replied, O Nebuchadnezzar, we do not need to answer you concerning this. Our God, whom we serve, is able to deliver us from the burning fiery furnace, and he will. But even if he does not save us, you must understand that we will not serve your gods or worship your golden image.

At this the King's face became dark with rage and he commanded that the furnace be heated seven times hotter than usual, and that his strongest soldiers bind Shadrach, Meshach and Abednego and cast them into the fire.

And so it was done. The heat of the furnace was so intense that the soldiers were burnt to death as Shadrach, Meshach and Abednego fell into the flames. Then the King jumped to his feet in

amazement and said to his advisors, Did we not cast three men into the fire? They answered, True, O King. But, he continued, I can see four men walking about in the midst of the fire, unhurt, and the fourth is like the Son of God.

Nebuchadnezzar came near the door of the burning fiery furnace and shouted, Shadrach, Meshach and Abednego, servants of the Most High God, come forth. And out they came from the heat of the fire. All who were gathered there saw that the fire had not touched them; their hair and clothes were not scorched and they did not smell of smoke.

Nebuchadnezzar said, Blessed be the God of Shadrach, Meshach and Abednego, who has sent his angel to deliver his servants who trusted in him. They defied the King's orders and faced death rather than serve or worship any god but their own. Therefore I make this decree: Men of all peoples, nations and languages! Anyone who speaks against the God of Shadrach, Meshach and Abednego will be cut in pieces and his house torn down, for there is no other God who can deliver like this.

Then the King promoted Shadrach, Meshach and Abednego, and they prospered in the province of Babylon.

Chapter 4

The proclamation of Nebuchadnezzar the King to men of every nation and language on earth;

Peace to you. It has seemed good to me to declare the signs and wonders that the Most High God has done for me.

How great are his signs,

How mighty his wonders,

His Kingdom is everlasting, and

His dominion is from generation to generation. I, Nebuchadnezzar, was at ease in my palace, and living in prosperity. I had a dream that made me fearful; the visions in my head alarmed me. I ordered all the wise men of Babylon to come before me and explain to me the meaning of the dream. Magicians, astrologers, Chaldeans and wizards came, and I told them what I had dreamt, but they could not interpret it for me. But at last Daniel came before me, whose Babylonian name was Belteshazzar and in whom the spirit of God Most Holy lives, and I told him the dream, saying, O Belteshazzar, chief of magicians, I know the spirit of the holy gods is in you, and no mystery is too great for you. This is my dream; tell me what it means.

These are the visions in my head as I lay on my bed. I saw a mighty tree in the midst of the earth. It grew large and strong, its top reached the sky, and it could be seen from the ends of the earth. Its leaves were beautiful and its fruit abundant; it provided shade for the beasts of the field, and the birds rested in it, and all living creatures fed themselves from it.

Next an angel, a holy one, came down from heaven and shouted, Chop down the tree and cut off its branches; strip off its leaves and scatter its fruit; let the beasts and the birds flee. But leave the stump with its roots in the ground, and with a band of iron and bronze around it in the grass of the field. Let him be wet with dew, let him share the grass with the animals, let him have the mind of a beast, and let seven times pass over him!

This is the decree of the angel seen by the King, the holy one from heaven, so that all alive may know that the Most High rules over the kingdoms of this world, and gives them to whom he pleases, even the lowliest of men.

This dream I, Nebuchadnezzar the King, have seen. Now you, Belteshazzar, tell me its meaning, since none of the wise men in my kingdom can interpret it. However, you will be able, for the spirit of the holy gods is in you.

Daniel sat stunned and silent for a while and his thoughts troubled him. The King said, Belteshazzar, do not be alarmed by the dream and its meaning.

Belteshazzar answered, My Lord, let the dream apply to your enemies and its interpretation to those who hate you!

The tree you saw, so tall and strong that it reached the sky, the tree with beautiful foliage and abundant fruit, the tree that provided food and shelter for all, that tree, O King, is you. You have become great and

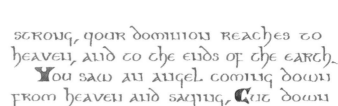

strong, your dominion reaches to heaven, and to the ends of the earth.

You saw an angel coming down from heaven and saying, Cut down the tree and destroy it, but leave the stump bound with bronze and iron in the grass of the field. Let him be wet with dew and eat grass with the animals until seven times passes over him. The meaning of this, and the decree of the Most High which has come upon you, is as follows: You will be driven away from human society and live with the beasts of the field and eat grass like the oxen and be wet with the dew of heaven for seven years, until you learn that the Most High is ruler over the kingdoms

of men, and gives power to whom he chooses. The command to leave the stump with its roots means your kingdom will be restored after you recognize that it is heaven that rules all.

O King, hear me. Break with your sins by righteous living, show mercy to the poor, and perhaps the Most High God will spare you.

But all this happened to King Nebuchadnezzar. Twelve months later he was walking on the roof of his royal palace, and he said, Great Babylon! Royal city which was built by me alone, in my mighty power and the glory of my majesty! And while he was speaking, a voice came from heaven:

King Nebuchadnezzar, these words are for you; you are to be driven out to eat grass with the animals; you will be wet with dew for seven years, until you realize that the Most High rules in the affairs of men.

And that same hour, the words came true. Nebuchadnezzar left the palace, ate grass with the oxen, and was wet with dew; his hair grew as long as eagle feathers, and his nails like bird's claws.

But after seven years, I, Nebuchadnezzar, lifted my eyes toward heaven, and my mind was restored, and I blessed the Most High, and praised him who lives for ever, whose rule is eternal, and whose kingdom lasts from age to age. All of the people on earth are as nothing compared to him; his will is done on earth and in heaven and no one can question it.

When my reason returned, my kingdom and former greatness were restored to me, and now I praise, glorify and honor the King of Heaven, whose works are true, whose promises are faithful, and who has the power to humble the proud.

Chapter 5

King Belshazzar gave a great banquet for a thousand of his nobles, and he drank wine in their company. While he was drinking he remembered the gold and silver vessels which his father Nebuchadnezzar had taken long ago from the temple in Jerusalem. He ordered his servants to bring in these sacred cups, and he and his nobles, wives and concubines drank wine from them and praised their idols of gold, silver, brass, iron, wood and stone.

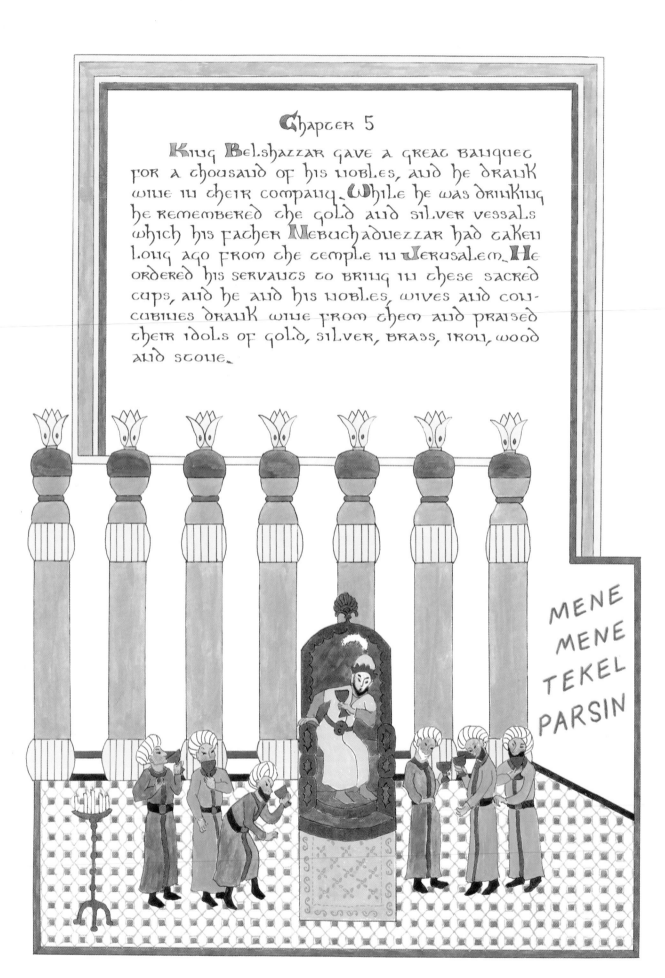

MENE
MENE
TEKEL
PARSIN

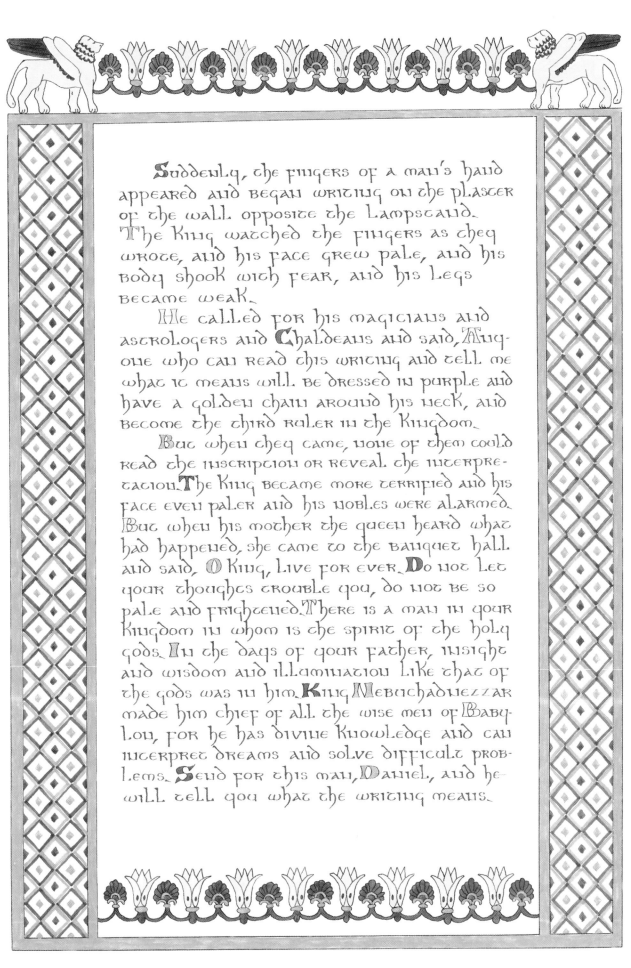

Suddenly, the fingers of a man's hand appeared and began writing on the plaster of the wall opposite the lampstand. The King watched the fingers as they wrote, and his face grew pale, and his body shook with fear, and his legs became weak.

He called for his magicians and astrologers and Chaldeans and said, Anyone who can read this writing and tell me what it means will be dressed in purple and have a golden chain around his neck, and become the third ruler in the kingdom.

But when they came, none of them could read the inscription or reveal the interpretation. The King became more terrified and his face even paler and his nobles were alarmed. But when his mother the queen heard what had happened, she came to the banquet hall and said, O King, live for ever. Do not let your thoughts trouble you, do not be so pale and frightened. There is a man in your kingdom in whom is the spirit of the holy gods. In the days of your father, insight and wisdom and illumination like that of the gods was in him. King Nebuchadnezzar made him chief of all the wise men of Babylon, for he has divine knowledge and can interpret dreams and solve difficult problems. Send for this man, Daniel, and he will tell you what the writing means.

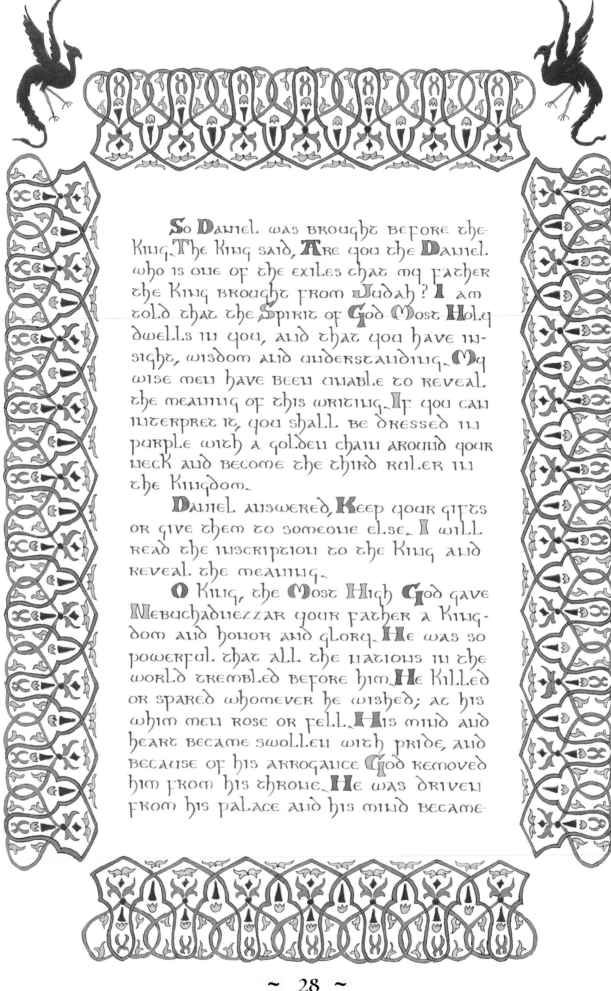

So Daniel was brought before the King. The King said, Are you the Daniel who is one of the exiles that my father the King brought from Judah? I am told that the Spirit of God Most Holy dwells in you, and that you have insight, wisdom and understanding. My wise men have been unable to reveal the meaning of this writing. If you can interpret it, you shall be dressed in purple with a golden chain around your neck and become the third ruler in the Kingdom.

Daniel answered, Keep your gifts or give them to someone else. I will read the inscription to the King and reveal the meaning.

O King, the Most High God gave Nebuchadnezzar your father a Kingdom and honor and glory. He was so powerful that all the nations in the world trembled before him. He killed or spared whomever he wished; at his whim men rose or fell. His mind and heart became swollen with pride, and because of his arrogance God removed him from his throne. He was driven from his palace and his mind became

like that of an animal. He ate grass with the oxen and was wet with the dew of heaven, until he recognized that the Most High rules in the affairs of men, and appoints whom he chooses to rule over them.

But you, Belshazzar, who are his son, know all this and yet have not been humble. You have defied the Lord of heaven, used the sacred vessals from his house to drink wine and praise your idols, gods who do not see or hear or know anything, and you do not praise the God who holds your life and breath in his hands. That is why he sent the hand to write this message: Mene, Mene, Tekel, and Parsin.

The meaning of the words is this: Mene - God has numbered the days of your kingdom and ended it; Tekel - you have been weighed in the balances and found wanting; Parsin - your kingdom has been divided and given to the Medes and the Persians.

At Belshazzar's command, Daniel was robed in purple, a golden chain was put around his neck, and he was proclaimed third in the kingdom. And that very night Belshazzar was killed, and Darius the Mede received the kingdom.

Chapter 6

King Darius appointed a hundred and twenty governors over the kingdom, and three presidents to oversee them, one of whom was Daniel. Because of his marvelous spirit and great ability, the king preferred Daniel over all the others, and planned to designate him ruler over the whole kingdom. The other governors were jealous and began looking for some way to discredit Daniel, but he was so honest and faultless that no criticism could be found.

So these men agreed that they could never discredit Daniel unless it had something to do with the law of his God. They decided to go to the king and say, King Darius, live forever. All of the governors have consulted together that you should issue the following decree: For the next thirty days whoever prays to any god or man, other than yourself, should be thrown into the lions' den. O king, sign this document so it may not be changed, for the law of the Medes and Persians cannot be revoked. And King Darius signed the decree.

When Daniel knew that the document had been signed, he went to his house. The windows of his upstairs room faced toward Jerusalem, and he knelt and prayed and gave thanks to God, as was his custom three times a day. These men came and found Daniel praying. They returned to the king and said, Did you not sign a decree forbidding prayer to any god or man other than yourself for thirty days, with those disobedient to be thrown into the lions' den?

The king replied, This is true, and the law of the Medes and Persians cannot be changed.

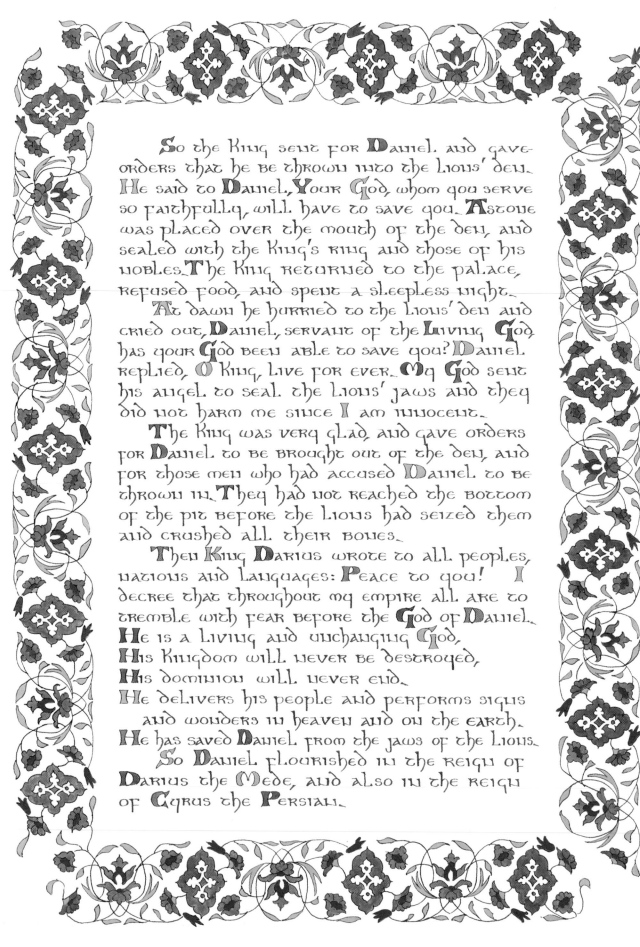

So the King sent for Daniel, and gave orders that he be thrown into the Lions' den. He said to Daniel, Your God, whom you serve so faithfully, will have to save you. A stone was placed over the mouth of the den, and sealed with the King's ring and those of his nobles. The King returned to the palace, refused food, and spent a sleepless night.

At dawn he hurried to the Lions' den and cried out, Daniel, servant of the Living God, has your God been able to save you? Daniel replied, O King, live for ever. My God sent his angel to seal the Lions' jaws and they did not harm me since I am innocent.

The King was very glad, and gave orders for Daniel to be brought out of the den, and for those men who had accused Daniel to be thrown in. They had not reached the bottom of the pit before the Lions had seized them and crushed all their bones.

Then King Darius wrote to all peoples, nations and languages: Peace to you! I decree that throughout my empire all are to tremble with fear before the God of Daniel. He is a Living and unchanging God, His Kingdom will never be destroyed, His dominion will never end. He delivers his people and performs signs and wonders in heaven and on the earth. He has saved Daniel from the jaws of the Lions.

So Daniel flourished in the reign of Darius the Mede, and also in the reign of Cyrus the Persian.

Chapter 7

In the first year of Belshazzar's reign as King of Babylon, Daniel had a dream which he wrote down. This is how he described the visions:

I saw the four winds of heaven stirring up the great sea; four great beasts came up out of the water, each different from the other.

The first beast was like a lion with eagle's wings. As I watched, its wings were torn off, and it was lifted from the ground and set upon two feet like a man, and a human heart was given to it.

The second beast was like a bear ready to strike, and it had three ribs in its mouth. I heard a voice cry, Up, devour much flesh.

The third beast was like a leopard which had wings on its back and four heads, and it was given great power.

Then the fourth beast rose out of the sea, most dreadful and terrible to look upon, and exceedingly strong. It had great iron teeth, and it tore its victims apart and crushed them under its feet. It was more vicious than the other beasts and it had ten horns. As I was looking at the horns, a small horn appeared, and three of the others were pulled out to make room for it. This little horn had human eyes and a mouth uttering boasts.

As I watched, thrones were set in place, and the Ancient of Days took his seat. His robe was white as snow, his hair was as pure wool, his throne was like fire and had flaming wheels. A river of fire poured out from before him. Thousands upon thousands ministered to him, and ten thousand times ten thousand stood before him in judgement and the books were opened.

As I gazed into the night visions, Behold, I saw coming on the clouds of heaven one like the Son of man. He came up to the Ancient of Days and was presented to him. He was given dominion, glory and power over the whole earth, that all people should serve him, and his kingdom shall last for ever.

I, Daniel, was troubled by these visions, and approached one of those standing near and asked the meaning of all this. This is what he said.

The four great beasts are four kings who will rise from the earth, but at the end the saints of the Most High will take the kingdom and possess it for ever and ever.

Then I asked about the fourth beast with iron teeth and bronze claws and ten horns. He said, The fourth beast is to be a fourth world kingdom different from the other kingdoms. From it will come another king, the little horn, who is even more brutal, and he will war against the saints of the Most High and defy God. His power will be broken at the coming of the Son of man, and his body committed to the flames. And then every nation on earth will belong to the people of God.

That was the end of the dream and I was greatly disturbed, but I spoke to no one about it.

Chapter 8

In the third year of the reign of Belshazzar, King of Babylon, I, Daniel, had another dream similar to the first. In it I was at the citadel at Susa, capital of the province of Elam, standing by the river Ulai. Looking around, I saw a ram with two long horns on the river bank. One of the horns grew longer than the other. The ram butted everything out of his way, no animal could stand before him or help his victims. He was very powerful.

Suddenly a male goat appeared from the west, so fast he flew over the ground. He had one large horn between his eyes. He charged the ram and broke off both of his horns, and the ram fell to the ground helpless and was trampled. The male goat grew strong and proud, but then his large horn was broken off and four smaller horns replaced it.

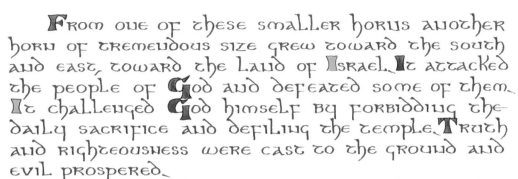

From one of these smaller horns another horn of tremendous size grew toward the south and east, toward the land of Israel. It attacked the people of God and defeated some of them. It challenged God himself by forbidding the daily sacrifice and defiling the temple. Truth and righteousness were cast to the ground and evil prospered.

As I, Daniel, was trying to understand this vision, I saw before me someone who looked like a man. Then a voice called out from across the river, Gabriel, tell Daniel the meaning of the dream. He came closer to me and I sank to the ground in fear. He said, Son of man, this vision pertains to end times. When he spoke I fainted and fell forward on my face. However, he touched me and raised me to my feet. I am here, he said, to explain the dream and to tell you what is to happen in the future.

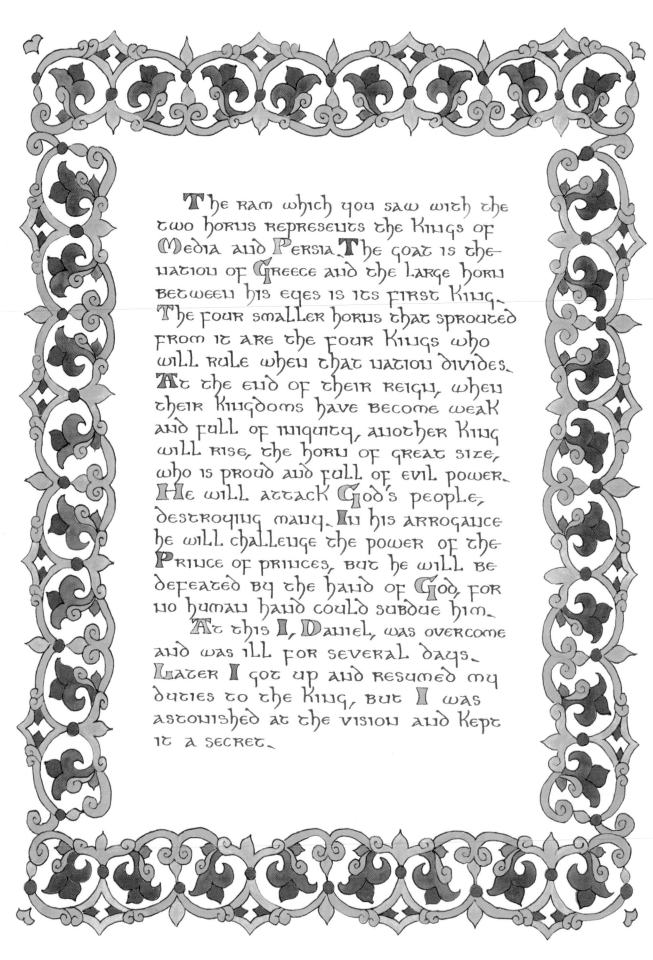

The ram which you saw with the two horns represents the Kings of Media and Persia. The goat is the nation of Greece and the large horn between his eyes is its first King. The four smaller horns that sprouted from it are the four Kings who will rule when that nation divides. At the end of their reign, when their Kingdoms have become weak and full of iniquity, another King will rise, the horn of great size, who is proud and full of evil power. He will attack God's people, destroying many. In his arrogance he will challenge the power of the Prince of princes, but he will be defeated by the hand of God, for no human hand could subdue him.

At this I, Daniel, was overcome and was ill for several days. Later I got up and resumed my duties to the king, but I was astonished at the vision and kept it a secret.

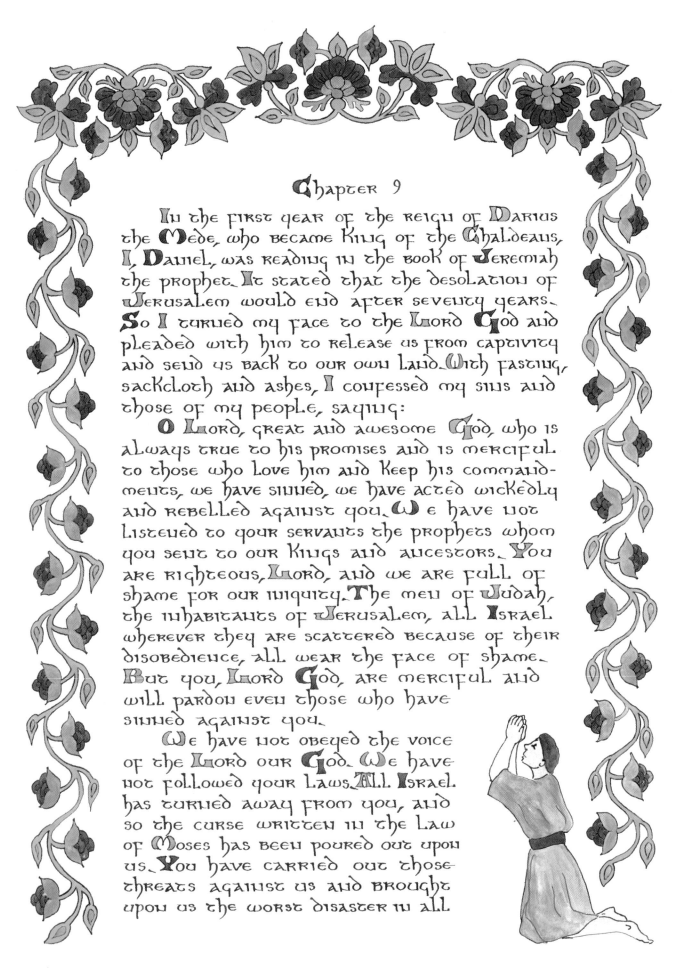

Chapter 9

In the first year of the reign of Darius the Mede, who became king of the Chaldeans, I, Daniel, was reading in the book of Jeremiah the prophet. It stated that the desolation of Jerusalem would end after seventy years. So I turned my face to the Lord God and pleaded with him to release us from captivity and send us back to our own land. With fasting, sackcloth and ashes, I confessed my sins and those of my people, saying:

O Lord, great and awesome God, who is always true to his promises and is merciful to those who love him and keep his commandments, we have sinned, we have acted wickedly and rebelled against you. We have not listened to your servants the prophets whom you sent to our kings and ancestors. You are righteous, Lord, and we are full of shame for our iniquity. The men of Judah, the inhabitants of Jerusalem, all Israel wherever they are scattered because of their disobedience, all wear the face of shame. But you, Lord God, are merciful and will pardon even those who have sinned against you.

We have not obeyed the voice of the Lord our God. We have not followed your laws. All Israel has turned away from you, and so the curse written in the law of Moses has been poured out upon us. You have carried out those threats against us and brought upon us the worst disaster in all the world. Even so we have not turned from our sins and followed your truth. Because you are just this calamity has come upon us.

You, Lord God, delivered your people from Egypt with a strong hand, bringing great honor to your name. Now, Lord, turn away your anger from us and from Jerusalem, your holy city, for because of our sins we have become a reproach to all those around us. Now, hear the prayer of your servant and for your own glory let your face shine again upon your desolate people.

O Lord God, hear our plea. Open your eyes and see our desolation; we ask not because of any merit of ours, but because of your great mercy. Hear us, Lord, forgive us, Lord. Listen, Lord, and act. For your own sake, Lord God, do not delay because we and your holy city are called by your name.

And while I was praying and confessing my sin and the sins of my people, Gabriel, whom I had seen in the earlier vision, suddenly flew down and touched me. He said, Daniel, I have come to help you understand God's plan for Israel. At the moment

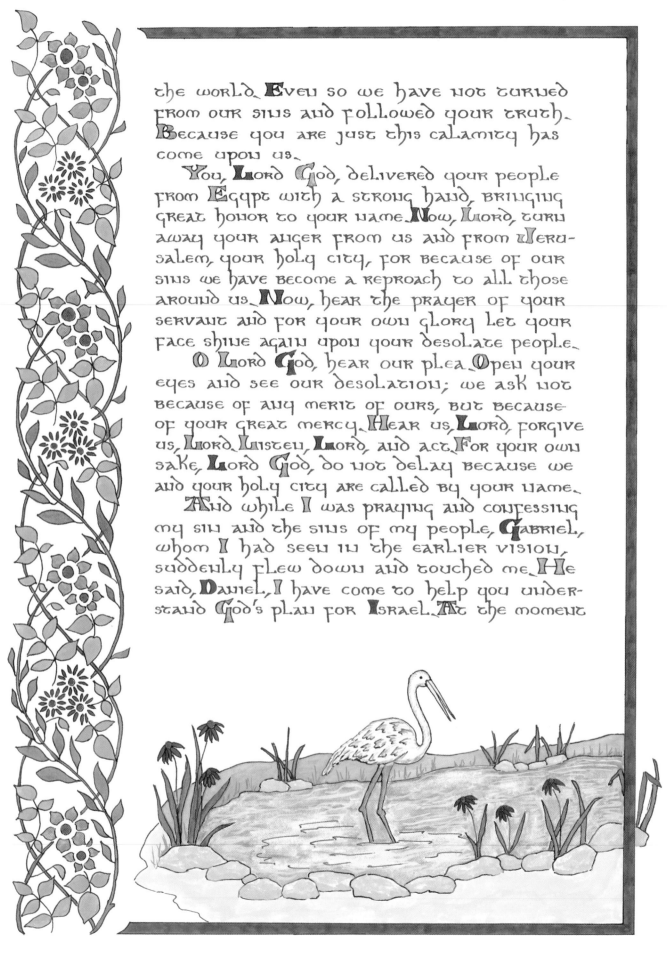

you began praying, a command was given, and I have come to tell you what it was, for you are greatly beloved.

Seventy times seven years are decreed for your people to finish the transgression, to make an end of sin, to atone for iniquity, to bring in everlasting righteousness, to seal up the vision and prophecy, and to anoint the most Holy.

Hear me. From the issuing of a message to return and rebuild Jerusalem until the coming of Messiah Prince will be sixty-nine times seven years. The city will be built again with walls and streets. At the end of sixty-two times seven years, the Messiah will be cut off, his Kingdom yet unrealized, and the people of a later prince will destroy the city and temple. They in turn will be overcome by war as God's judgment is poured out upon them.

Chapter 10

In the third year of Cyrus King of Persia another vision was given to Daniel. It was a true revelation of great conflict to come.

In those days I, Daniel, was in mourning for three weeks. I ate no pleasant bread and had no wine or meat, nor did I anoint myself.

On the twenty-fourth day of the first month I was standing on the bank of the great Tigris river when, looking up, I beheld a man clothed in white linen with a belt of pure gold. His face shone, his eyes were like flames, his arms and feet gleamed like bronze and his voice was like a multitude.

I alone saw the vision, the men who were with me did not, however they were suddenly filled with dread and ran away. I was alone with this vision. I grew pale and all my strength left me. He spoke to me and I fell forward in a deep sleep. Then he touched me and lifted me to my hands and knees. He said, Daniel, greatly beloved of God, understand what you hear, stand up and listen, for I have been sent to you. So I rose, trembling. He said, Daniel, fear not. From the first day of your fast the Lord heard your prayer and answered it, and sent me to you. I have come to tell you what will happen to your people in the latter days. When he said this I looked at the ground, speechless. Then someone touched my lips and I was able to say, My Lord, I am overcome at this vision and have no strength to speak. How can I, your servant, speak to you, my Lord, when there is no breath left in me. Then he touched me again and I felt stronger. He said, O man, greatly beloved of God, fear not. Peace be unto you. Be strong. I have come to tell you what is written in the Book of Truth.

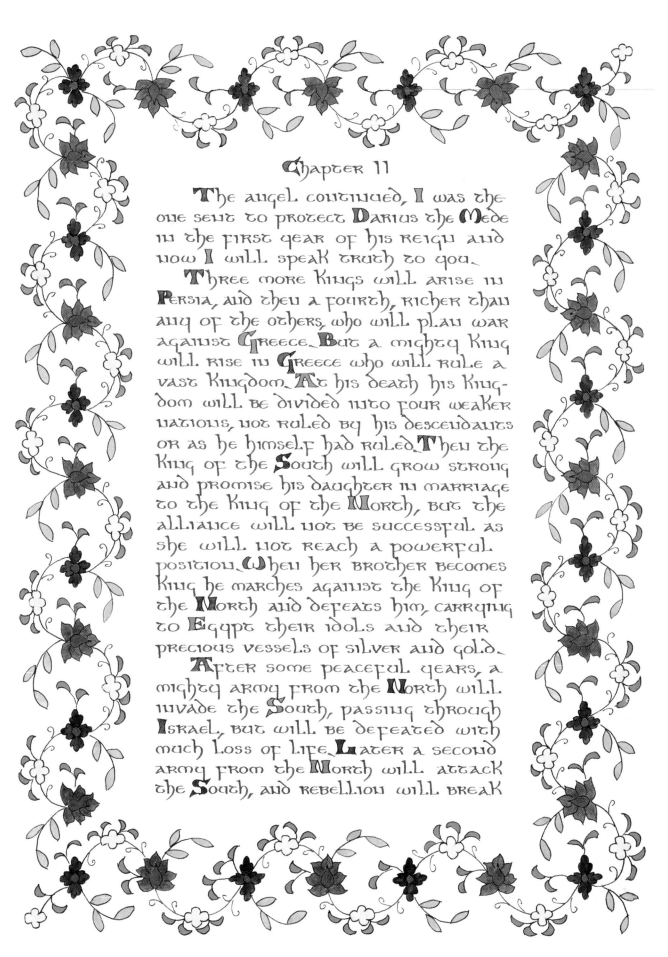

Chapter 11

The angel continued, I was the one sent to protect Darius the Mede in the first year of his reign and now I will speak truth to you.

Three more kings will arise in Persia, and then a fourth, richer than any of the others, who will plan war against Greece. But a mighty king will rise in Greece who will rule a vast kingdom. At his death his kingdom will be divided into four weaker nations, not ruled by his descendants or as he himself had ruled. Then the king of the South will grow strong and promise his daughter in marriage to the king of the North, but the alliance will not be successful as she will not reach a powerful position. When her brother becomes king he marches against the king of the North and defeats him, carrying to Egypt their idols and their precious vessels of silver and gold.

After some peaceful years, a mighty army from the North will invade the South, passing through Israel, but will be defeated with much loss of life. Later a second army from the North will attack the South, and rebellion will break out against the King of the South. A seige against a fortified city of Egypt will cause these armies to be defeated, and the victorious King of the North will also plunder Israel as he moves to conquer all Egypt.

A succession of evil rulers will ascend the throne of the North, laying waste to the lands of the South and putting godless men in power in Jerusalem. Those with spiritual understanding will speak, but will be brought down by sword, flame and captivity. The greatest of these northern kings will do as he pleases, claiming to be greater than every god and blaspheming the God of gods until what has been decreed by God against him is fulfilled. He will come to his end as his royal tents are pitched between the sea and Jerusalem.

Chapter 12

The angel continued, At that time Michael, that mighty prince who stands guard over your people, will arise. There will be a time of great distress in the land, but those whose names are written in the Book of Life will be spared. Many of those who sleep in the dust of the earth will awake, some to everlasting life and others to shame and everlasting disgrace. Those who are wise will shine as the brightness of the firmament, and those who turn many to righteousness will be bright as stars. But you, Daniel, must keep these words secret, and keep the book sealed until the time of the end when travel and knowledge will greatly increase.

Then I, Daniel, looked and saw two others on each bank of the river. One said to the man dressed in linen, How long will it be until these wonders take place? And the man dressed in linen raised both hands toward heaven and swore by Him that lives for ever that it would be a time, times and half a time after he who shatters the power of God's people meets his end.

I heard this but did not understand, so I asked, O my Lord, how will all this end?

He replied, Go your way, Daniel, these words are sealed until the time of the end. Many will be purified, but the wicked, not understanding, will go on doing wrong, but those who are wise will understand. Blessed is he who stands firm. As for you, go on to the end. You will enter into rest and rise again at the end of time.